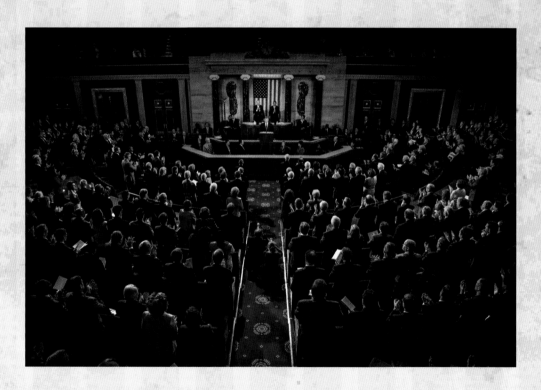

The Bill of Rights

LIMITING FEDERAL POWERS

THE TENTH AMENDMENT

Hallie Murray

Enslow Publishing
101 W. 23rd Street
Suite 240
New York, NY 10011
USA

enslow.com

Published in 2018 by Enslow Publishing, LLC.
101 W. 23rd Street, Suite 240, New York, NY 10011

Library of Congress Cataloging-in-Publication Data

Names: Murray, Hallie, author.
Title: Limiting federal powers : the Tenth Amendment / Hallie Murray.
Description: New York, NY : Enslow Publishing, 2018. | Series: The bill of
  rights | Includes bibliographical references and index.
Identifiers: LCCN 2017001922 | ISBN 9780766085671 (library-bound) | ISBN
  9780766087453 (pbk.) | ISBN 9780766087460 (6-pack)
Subjects: LCSH: United States. Constitution. 10th
  Amendment—History—Juvenile literature. | Federal government—United
  States—History—Juvenile literature. | States' rights (American
  politics)—History—Juvenile literature.
Classification: LCC KF4558 10th .M87 2017 | DDC 342.73/042—dc23
LC record available at https://lccn.loc.gov/2017001922

Printed in China

To Our Readers: We have done our best to make sure all website addresses in this book were active and appropriate when we went to press. However, the author and the publisher have no control over and assume no liability for the material available on those websites or on any websites they may link to. Any comments or suggestions can be sent by e-mail to customerservice@enslow.com.

Portions of this book originally appeared in the book *The Tenth Amendment: Limiting Federal Powers* by Tamra Orr.

Photo Credits: Cover, p. 1 Drop of Light/Shutterstock.com; cover, interior pages (background) A-R-T/Shutterstock.com; cover, interior pages (quill) Leporska Lyubov/ Shutterstock.com; p. 5 Chip Somodevilla/Getty Images; p. 9 DEA Picture Library/De Agostini/Getty Images; p. 11 Culture Club/Hulton Archive/Getty Images; p. 13 Universal History Archive/Universal Images Group/Getty Images; p. 14 Bettmann/Getty Images; p. 19 Bill Perry/Shutterstock.com; pp. 21, 24 Library of Congress; p. 27 Stock Montage/ Archive Photos/Getty Images; p. 29 Universal Images Group/Getty Images; p. 32 Andy Sacks/Photographer's Choice/Getty Images; p. 38 © AP Images; p. 40 ATF/Getty Images.

Contents

INTRODUCTION

In 1996, the Defense of Marriage Act (DOMA) was passed. It ruled that marriage, for federal purposes, meant only the union of one man and one woman. It didn't prohibit gay marriage, but it did allow married same-sex couples to be denied federal benefits given to spouses. It also meant that states did not have to recognize same-sex marriages that had happened in other states.

In 2013, DOMA was ruled unconstitutional in the Supreme Court Case *United States v. Windsor*. Edith Windsor and Thea Spyer were a same-sex couple living in New York who had gotten married in Toronto in 2007. In 2009, at the age of 78, Spyer died, leaving everything she had to her wife, Windsor. Inheritance like that is usually taxed, but Windsor asked for the exemption usually given to spouses. She was denied because the United States government would not recognize that she had been Spyer's wife. Windsor sued and won, and Section 3 of DOMA was ruled unconstitutional because it violated the Fifth Amendment.

While *United States v. Windsor* was successful thanks to the Fifth Amendment, many conversations about the unconstitutionality of DOMA cited other amendments and aspects of the constitution. If Windsor had not won, another of these cases would surely

Edith Windsor raises her hands in celebration and acknowledges her supporters after successfully winning her Supreme Court Case over DOMA.

have made it to the Supreme Court—DOMA seems to have been unconstitutional in a number of ways. *Massachusetts v. United States Department of Health and Human Services*, a 2009 case decided by the First Circuit's (New England's) Court of Appeals, ruled that in fact DOMA was unconstitutional because it was a case of the government overstepping its bounds and taking on powers not allotted to it. It was a case about the Tenth Amendment.

The Tenth Amendment is one of the least understood—and therefore the most debated—amendments in the Bill of Rights, which are the first ten amendments to the Constitution. Unlike the first eight, both the Ninth and Tenth amendments do not spell out specific, concrete rights that are easy to identify and name. These two amendments are much more abstract and vague in their wording. This has caused a great deal of trouble since they were first ratified in the late eighteenth century.

The Tenth Amendment states, "The powers not delegated to the United States by the Constitution, not prohibited by it to the States, are reserved for the States respectively, or to the people." What does this mean? It states a simple truth: There are powers that belong to the federal government, but those that do not belong to the federal government belong to the individual states and the people who live in them. Of course, people argue aobut the specific meanings of different phrases, but the heart of the matter stays the same.

The Tenth Amendment was put in place to remind the federal government that states and their residents had important rights that could not be taken away. This was a constitutional assurance that the people of this newly formed nation required. After all, individual rights and self-rule were what the American colonists had been battling Britain for both before and during the American Revolution. These were ideals that many Americans had sacrificed their safety, security, homes, and even lives to gain. They weren't about to let a government of their own choosing take away what had been so hard fought for and dearly won.

CHAPTER ONE

UNITING *the* STATES UNDER *a* FEDERAL GOVERNMENT

In 1776, the citizens of the American colonies first declared their desire to become independent from Britain. In 1783, they finally gained their independence and escaped the tyrannical rule of the British king and parliament. The citizens of this new nation, the United States of America, were excited and eager to start their new lives as free and self-governing American citizens, but with this new freedom came great responsibility. Creating a new government that would rule wisely and fairly was much harder than criticizing and rebelling against an existing government.

During the American Revolutionary War, the thirteen colonies remained largely united because they all shared the same goal: independence from Britain. Once they had gained that, however, they found themselves struggling with a whole new set of problems, including the creation of a government for their new country. They already knew that they did not want to replicate the governments of any existing nations, but they weren't sure what they *did* want. Finally, after many debates and discussions, they made some important decisions about their new country.

Some of the models used for the new American government were the governments of ancient Greek and Roman communities. This is where the earliest Americans got the idea to make the new nation a republic, or a government that was based on the will and consent of the people. To that end, they wanted a leader that would be elected on their merits and abilities and not because of royal heritage, an influential family, wealth, or powerful connections. They wanted a government that would give the nation and society structure by uniting the states, but one that wouldn't have the power to control their personal and private lives. Finding this balance was not easily achieved.

THE FAILURE OF THE ARTICLES OF CONFEDERATION

The first document that attempted to outline the powers and structure of the new country's federal government was the Articles of Confederation. Drafted in 1777, it was ratified four years later. The Articles of Confederation established a permanent national congress made up of from between two and seven delegates each of the thirteen states.

Regarding what powers the federal government had as compared to states' rights, Article II of the document declared that "each state retains its sovereignty, freedom, and independence, and every power, jurisdiction, and right, which is not by this Confederacy expressly delegated to the United States, in Congress assembled." This meant that any power not explicitly reserved for the federal government in the Articles of Confederation automatically belonged to the states. The federal government—which consisted only of Congress at this point—had very few powers granted to it. So the states retained many rights and enormous governing power under the Articles of Confederation.

Yet it soon became apparent that in order to properly govern the country, the Federal government would need more power than was granted to it by the Articles of Confederation. The clamor for changes to the Articles of Confederation grew,

George Washington signs the Constitution as a delegate from Virginia at the 1787 convention in Philadelphia.

and finally during the summer of 1787, fifty-five delegates from the thirteen states met in Philadelphia, Pennsylvania to address these issues. They gathered to determine how to create a document that provided for a stronger, more effective federal government, and finally they came up with the document that still governs the United States—the Constitution.

THE UNITED STATES CONSTITUTION IS BORN

It took almost four months for thirty-nine of the fifty-five delegates to sign the final draft of the Constitution. Now, nine of the thirteen states would have to ratify the document for it to go into effect. On June 21, 1788, New Hampshire became the ninth state to ratify the Constitution. Eight months later, it went into effect. By 1790, all thirteen of the original states had ratified the US Constitution. A major argument developed between Federalists and Anti-Federalists over the rights of individuals.

This remarkable document consisted of two parts: the introduction, often referred to as the Preamble, and the body, composed of seven sections called Articles. These Articles describe legislative power, executive power, judicial power, states' powers and limits, the amendment process, federal power, and the ratification process. Yet many people felt that while the Constitution was a good start, it did not provide enough protection for average citizens against potential government abuse.

Their anxiety was easy to understand. After all they had lived under tyrannical British rule, the people in this new nation insisted upon a better government than

This map displays the thirteen original colonies of the United States *(in pink)*. At the time, Spain owned Florida and France owned the land west of the colonies. In 1803, the United States bought this land from France in the Louisiana Purchase.

what they had during the colonial era. While they had been waiting for a national constitution, the states had already formed individual declarations that included the freedom of speech, freedom of the press, and the right to a trial by a jury for their citizens. State delegates wanted to see a similar bill of rights built into the Constitution.

A DEMOCRATIC REPUBLIC

Many people simply refer to the United States as a democracy, but it is actually a "democratic republic," meaning that it is both a democracy and a republic. A democracy is a form of government where power lies with the citizens, who make decisions based on majority vote or elect representatives to office to make decisions for them. A republic is a sovereign state where people are governed by elected officials, but not everyone might get to vote. A sovereign state is a group of people living in a specific place that rules themselves, like the countries we see today. Not all democracies are sovereign states. The Founding Fathers did not necessarily approve of direct democracy, where every citizen gets to vote on every issue, which is why they made America a republic as well as a democracy. James Madison, the main author of the Constitution, argued in Federalist Paper No. 10 that a democracy gets weaker when it gets bigger, because there are too many different opinions, but republics get stronger as they grow because they have fixed laws. In the United States, we have fixed laws that the people make, so we are a democratic republic.

The Bill of Rights

THE FEDERALIST PAPERS

During the two years that the Constitution was being drafted and debated, politicians did not have many ways to reach the American people and share their opinions and ideas. In the late eighteenth century, there was only one means of relatively fast mass communication: letters to the editors of city newspapers.

In the six months before the Constitution's ratification, a series of eighty-five letters were published in a number of New York newspapers. They were primarily written by the Federalists Alexander Hamilton, James Madison, and John Jay. Yet readers did not know the true identities of the writers; the letters were written under the pen name Publius. Each one of the letters and essays discussed in detail the many reasons why the new Constitution should be ratified.

At the same time, a number of other letters were written in response by Anti-Federalist authors who used pen names such as Cato, Centinel, Federal Farmer, and Brutus. These were also published in New York newspapers, and they detailed the reasons why the Constitution should be thoroughly questioned, analyzed, and amended before ratification.

John Jay was a Federalist and delegate from New York to the Continental Congress. Later on, he became secretary of state under George Washington and the first chief justice of the Supreme Court.

CREATING THE BILL OF RIGHTS

One of the major issues that Federalists and Anti-Federalists had argued about was whether or not the Constitution needed a bill of rights. Federalists argued that such rights were so obvious that they need not be stated, but Anti-Federalists pointed to the ways that Britain had violated the colonists' rights as evidence that they did. The Federalists were ultimately successful, but soon after the Constitution was signed,

Women who fought for the right to vote were called suffragettes, and here many suffragettes can be seen marching on Washington, DC, in 1913. The Fifteenth Amendment (1870) gave African American men the right to vote, and the Nineteenth Amendment (1920) gave women the right to vote.

its authors were forced to rethink their stance on the bill of rights due to pressure from Anti-Federalist state delegates.

As a result, a series of ten constitutional amendments, known collectively as the Bill of Rights, was proposed in 1789 and ratified in 1791. These amendments were created to address questions or rights missing or requiring clarification in the original Constitution. In the years since the Bill of Rights was ratified, another seventeen amendments to the Constitution have been passed into law. These later amendments tackle issues such as the abolition of slavery, voting rights for African Americans and women, the national voting age, and presidential term limits.

"BIG" GOVERNMENT VERSUS "SMALL" GOVERNMENT

The fierce debates and disagreements over the Constitution and the Bill of Rights among delegates to the Constitutional Convention exposed a major philosophical divide in America. On one side were those who felt that the federal government should serve as a strong central command with a great deal of power. This centralized power would help bind the states together and prevent chaos. Without a strong central government, it was argued, the United States would actually be a disunited collection of independent nation-states, each with its own set of laws and policies. The Federalists, as is clear from the Federalist Papers, believed in the importance of a strong central government. While today's Democratic Party is not the same as the Federalist

Party, both parties had similar beliefs about the importance of a "big" federal government.

On the other side were those who wanted to avoid any chance of ever living under a repressive and tyrannical government, and they became known as the Anti-Federalists, as they wrote the Anti-Federalist Papers in response to the Federalist Papers. They fought for a system in which the power to make decisions would mostly stay with the individual states. The Republican Party is the political party today that believes in the importance of "small" government. Of course, just like the Republicans and the Democrats, both sides in the discussion between Federalists and Anti-Federalists wanted what was best for their new country. It can just be hard to agree on what exactly that entails.

CHAPTER TWO

CLEAR DIVISIONS *and the* (IM)BALANCE *of* POWERS

After suffering under Britain's increasingly tyrannical leadership, Americans must have been happy to have a governing document that would protect their basic rights, like the right to free speech or the right to fair, speedy trials decided by a jury of peers. It is easy to understand why people fought so hard to add the first eight amendments to the Constitution. These amendments protect specific rights that the state representatives felt were important. Yet the Ninth and Tenth Amendments are different. Where the first eight amendments protect specific, individual rights, the two final amendments in the Bill of Rights are worded so as to cover "everything else." The Ninth Amendment protects all rights not stated in the Bill of Rights, and the Tenth Amendment limits the power of the federal government.

The Tenth Amendment says: "The powers not delegated to the United States by the Constitution, not prohibited by it to the States, are reserved for the States respectively, or to the people." This vague wording is the result of the emotion, anxiety, and fierce debate that went into it. For many Americans, the Tenth Amendment summarizes the intentions of the entire Constitution, because it defines, however vaguely, the powers that the federal government does and does not have. Tenth Amendment sought to express the limits of federal power, thereby identifying what rights belonged to the individual states and the people living within them. The idea that certain powers were retained by the states was key. The "United States of America" is named very intentionally. The states must be "united" by the federal government, but they also must remain states, with their own powers and responsibilities separate from one another.

STATES' RIGHTS AND THE BILL OF RIGHTS

As we learned in the last chapter, the Federalists were the group that believed the federal government should have a lot of power. They were led by such historical figures as Alexander Hamilton, John Jay, and future president James Madison, the three authors of the Federalist Papers. They were convinced that the best government for this new nation was a strong, centralized one. Otherwise, they believed, the states would slowly separate and the nation would fall apart. Businesspeople and bankers tended to rally behind them because the Federalists also favored the creation of a national bank and mint and sound national fiscal policies.

In one of the Federalist papers, Federalist No. 45, Madison writes, "The powers delegated by the proposed Constitution to the federal government are few and defined. Those which are to remain in the State governments are numerous and indefinite. The former [federal powers] will be exercised principally on external objects, as war, peace, negotiation, and foreign commerce; with which last the power of taxation will, for the most part, be connected." Madison strongly believed that this division of authority was created in order "to ensure protection of our fundamental liberties."

This statue of Alexander Hamilton stands in front of the United States Department of the Treasury. Hamilton was the very first United States secretary of the treasury and was instrumental in creating the first national bank.

Madison also added, "The powers reserved to the several States will extend to all the objects which, in the ordinary course of affairs, concern the lives, liberties, and properties of the people, and the internal order, improvement, and prosperity of the State." Given that the Constitution already created this clear division between a few important federal powers and all remaining powers delegated to the states, some Federalists did not quite understand the necessity for the Bill of Rights. Why take the time to outline in a series of amendments what the federal government could not do

THE DANGERS OF THE BILL OF RIGHTS

It can be difficult to understand why people would be against the Bill of Rights. Of course individuals should be guaranteed specific rights! Yet many people, especially the Federalists, felt that a Bill of Rights would be not only unnecessary but possibly also dangerous. In Federalist No. 84, Alexander Hamilton wrote, "For why declare that things shall not be done which there is no power to do?" Meaning that the federal government could not infringe on people's rights anyway, so it made no sense to write down specific rights and not others. Hamilton and other Federalists also worried that the Bill of Rights might actually cause people's rights to be violated. If these ten amendments that spelled out specific rights and protections were added to the Constitution, it might imply that any rights not specified would be considered unprotected or even unlawful. There were many unspoken rights that still needed protection! Hamilton and others thought that writing down just ten rights in the Bill of Rights would mean that the countless other rights granted to citizens would become meaningless.

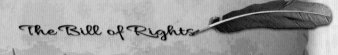

The Bill of Rights

when it was never empowered by the Constitution to do these things in the first place?

The Anti-Federalists, led by people such as Thomas Jefferson and Patrick Henry, believed that the Bill of Rights was an absolutely essential and necessary part of the Constitution. Jefferson believed that the Tenth Amendment was so important that he referred to it as "the foundation of the Constitution." Although the Anti-Federalists agreed that a Constitution was needed, they deeply feared one that would grant too much power to the federal government—power that rightfully belonged to the states and the American people. "The government which governs least, governs best," stated Jefferson.

THE TENTH AMENDMENT GOES TO COURT

The Tenth Amendment went to the heart of the Federalist/Anti-Federalist debate by attempting to identify the limits of federal power and delineate states' rights and the rights of the people. The amendment was designed to make the various layers of American government more efficient and less complicated, with fewer areas of overlap and dispute. In practice, however, it did just the opposite in many cases throughout history.

Thomas Jefferson was an Anti-Federalist, delegate from Virginia, ambassador to France, and the third President of the United States.

One of the first important court cases that tested the Tenth Amendment's attempted division of federal and state powers was *McCulloch v. Maryland* in 1819. At that time, the state of Maryland believed that the federal government did not have the power to establish a national bank because it wasn't listed as a right in the Constitution. Nevertheless, the US government had gone ahead and created the Second Bank of the United States, a national bank. It was based in Philadelphia but also opened a branch in Baltimore, Maryland, without that state's approval. In response, Maryland taxed the bank's operations and imposed fines for nonpayment of the tax. When branch manager James McCulloch refused to pay the taxes and fines, Maryland took the bank to court.

Eventually the case went all the way to the Supreme Court, which decided in favor of the federal government. According to Chief Justice John Marshall, creating a national bank with branches throughout the country encouraged business between states, and that was good for the entire country. In addition, Marshall stated that Maryland could not tax a "national entity." Marshall added, "Let the end be legitimate, let it be within the scope of the Constitution, and all means which are appropriate, which are plainly adapted to that end, which are not prohibited, but consistent with the letter and spirit of the Constitution, are constitutional."

What he meant was that if the ultimate goal is legitimate and constitutional—in this case, the establishment of a national bank—and all of the actions necessary to reach that goal are not in direct violation of the Constitution, then

INTERFERING FOR THE GOOD OF THE PEOPLE

One of the most influential court cases centering on the Tenth Amendment is *Hammer v. Dagenhart* (1918). It all began with child labor. Many children at that time worked. In fact, in some factories, almost half of the employees were between the ages of seven and sixteen years old. In the mid-1800s, child labor laws began to appear in different states in an effort to protect these young people, but the federal government stayed out of the issue, allowing the individual states to address it. The federal government could not interfere because it didn't have the constitutional right. Yet concern over child labor continued to grow, until finally two men named Edward Keating and Robert Owen located a loophole in the law that would allow federal intervention. Then they proposed the Child Labor Act of 1916. This act would prohibit (forbid) the interstate shipment of products made by businesses that employed children who were too young or worked too many hours. It made a lot of people mad. One North Carolina man, Roland Dagenhart, who worked in a cotton mill with his two teenaged sons, argued that the law was unconstitutional. He claimed the federal government was not empowered to tell people how to run their businesses. The case eventually reached the Supreme Court, where the US attorney for the Western District of North Carolina, W. C. Hammer, argued that the new child labor law was necessary to protect the public good. The court was divided 5–4, with the majority ruling in favor of Dagenhart. The nation's first child labor law was officially overturned.

The Bill of Rights

This picture from 1911 shows a number of children ages six to ten working in a canning factory in Mississippi. Poor children often worked long hours in dangerous factories instead of attending school.

those actions must also be considered constitutional. It was the first time the courts expressed the fact that the federal government had more powers than those few explicitly spelled out in the Constitution. In addition to its expressly stated powers, the Constitution provided the federal government with other, implied powers. The *McCulloch v. Maryland* decision also determined that when state and federal laws disagree, federal laws will win.

SLAVERY AND THE STATES

Several decades later, a national crisis developed over the issue of slavery that not only challenged the Tenth Amendment but also robbed it of its power for some time. Until the Civil War, most states preferred that the federal government allow them to make their own decisions regarding state business and local issues. This all changed when the antislavery movement began to gather strength. As federal legislation began to chip away at slaveholders' rights, the Southern states objected. The South was heavily dependent upon slave labor to work its cash crops of cotton, tobacco, and rice.

When Abraham Lincoln was elected president in 1860, the pressure to end slavery intensified. In protest, eleven Southern states seceded from the Union and formed the Confederate States of America. They believed that slavery was a state right—not a federal one. This disagreement resulted in the Civil War (1861–1865) and the creation of the Thirteenth Amendment, which abolished slavery throughout the country.

Although ending slavery was a noble goal for the nation, it came in direct conflict with the state powers provided by the Tenth Amendment. Because the Constitution failed to explicitly mention slavery and the federal government's right to regulate it, slave-holding seemed to fall under the category of states' rights guaranteed by the Tenth Amendment. For this reason, a constitutional amendment explicitly outlawing slavery in every state was required to get around this legal obstacle to federally mandated abolition.

CHAPTER THREE

The TENTH AMENDMENT in the TWENTIETH CENTURY

The controversy over the Tenth Amendment was far from over, however. Again and again, the issue of state versus federal powers would rear its head in cases throughout the country. And each time, it would raise the same question all over again: where do the federal government's powers end and states' rights begin?

As with most of the legal confusion and conflict that has surrounded the Bill of Rights, philosophical disagreements over the Tenth Amendment are almost always due to its ambiguous wording. The authors of the Constitution had to choose their words very carefully, but even the most carefully chosen phrasing can be read a number of ways. It's also possible they wanted the amendment to be ambiguous, so that it would be interpreted in the broadest possible way.

Another thing that makes understanding the amendment even more difficult is that some terms used in its wording seem to have changed meaning, though whether they actually have is often a matter of opinion more than anything else. The most important responsibility of the Supreme Court is interpreting the Constitution in the way that they think makes the most sense and is best for the country.

Although there have been court cases that challenged and explored the power of the Tenth Amendment over the years, the meaning and scope of the Tenth Amendment was not truly called into question until the 1930s. President Franklin D. Roosevelt's New Deal programs, which were created to solve the

Franklin Delano Roosevelt is widely considered one of the best presidents the United States has ever had, particularly by people in today's Democratic Party. He was a senator and governor in New York before becoming president in 1933. He is also the only president to ever serve more than two terms in office.

miserable conditions Americans faced during the Great Depression (1929–1941), stretched the limits of federal government powers further than ever before. Disagreements over the immense federal power invested in these important programs would put the Tenth Amendment to its greatest test yet.

THE NECESSARY NEW DEAL

Roosevelt was president of the United States when the nation and its people were literally struggling to survive. The depression had devastated the country. Unemployment soared. Families stood in line for food. Businesses were closing, and banks were unstable. During Roosevelt's presidential campaign, he had made great promises: "I pledge you, I pledge myself, to a New Deal for the American people… Give me your help, not to win votes alone, but to win in this crusade to restore America to its own people." The people were desperate for leadership and change. They looked to their government for help out of this catastrophe—and, in doing so, gave it more power than it had ever had before.

Roosevelt's campaign promises of a return to work and prosperity persuaded people to elect him president, and he quickly made good on his word. He created many New Deal programs designed to put the nation's people back to work. In the process, the country's infrastructure, natural environments, and culture were improved in many ways. The New Deal included programs that still exist today, such as the Federal Communications Commission (FCC), the Federal Deposit Insurance Corporation (FDIC), the Federal Housing Administration (FHA), and the Social Security Board. During his first term, Roosevelt created work for more than five million previously unemployed people.

Many people did not like New Deal policies because they felt that they were a waste of money. In this political cartoon from the 1930s, President Roosevelt pours more and more money down a leaky pipe so that most of it is wasted. This doesn't mean the New Deal policies really were finanically wasteful, but it does show that some people felt strongly that they were not working.

"GENERAL WELFARE" IN
SOUTH DAKOTA V. DOLE

There is general agreement throughout society, government, and the courts about the fact that underage drinking is illegal and unacceptable. Yet there have been surprisingly bitter constitutional debates about what constitutes "underage" and who gets to decide what a state's legal drinking age should be. In 1984, Congress passed legislation called the National Minimum Drinking Age Act. It stated that 5 percent of Federal Aid Highway Act money would be withheld from any state that did not adopt a minimum legal drinking age of twenty-one, because drunk driving was thought of as a national issue. This meant that a state would not receive the funds necessary to build and maintain its federal interstate highways.

This new federal rule made the legislature of South Dakota very angry. The state normally sold beer to nineteen year olds, but it could not afford to lose its federal highway funds. The state decided to sue, naming Secretary of Transportation Elizabeth Dole as defendant because it was her department that enforced this new legislation. In *South Dakota v. Dole*, the Supreme Court ruled that Congress was allowed to set the national drinking age under the Taxing and Spending Clause because it was for the "general welfare" of American citizens. It also ruled that the act did not violate the Tenth Amendment as South Dakota claimed because states were being "pressured" to comply with it but were not absolutely required to.

The Bill of Rights

However, not every New Deal program was a success or even enjoyed popular, political, or legal support. Altogether almost a dozen of Roosevelt's New Deal programs were declared unconstitutional by the Supreme Court because they tried to use federal power to overrule the policies of state governments. The Supreme Court declared in these decisions that if a state had a crisis, it was to take care of it on its own, instead of relying on a federal program or other forms of assistance. Federal issues, like widespread poverty caused by the Great Depression, could be dealt with using federal programming. Yet it could be difficult to tell which issues belonged to the states and which belonged to the nation as a whole. Each time one of these New Deal programs was called into question, it reminded people that the wording of the Tenth Amendment was often open to interpretation and confusion.

THREE CLAUSES FOR CONGRESS

As time has passed, especially in the wake of Progressive Era regulatory reform in the early twentieth century and Roosevelt's massive New Deal program, the federal government has developed a great deal of control over areas of national scope and importance, including agriculture, the manufacturing industry, and labor unions. Some of these gains have occurred due to reinterpretations of the Tenth Amendment, but many have occurred thanks to reinterpretations of the powers actually granted to the federal government by the Constitution. After all, the Tenth Amendment, at its simplest, says that the government has all powers granted to it by the

These wheat harvesters are one of the many different pieces of the farming and agriculture industry responsible for providing Americans with food and fuel.

Constitution and none else. Much of this constitutionally-based power is granted by three specific clauses found in Article 1, Section 8 of the Constitution.

The Commerce Clause

The Commerce Clause has been dissected and analyzed a great deal since the Constitution's framers first wrote it. It states that "Congress shall have power to regulate commerce with foreign nations and among the several states, and with the Indian Tribes." Some experts claim that the Constitutional Convention delegates used the word "commerce" to mean nothing more than trade. Others believe they meant it to encompass all economic activities. If the latter is true, the clause gives the government freedom to regulate almost all aspects of American business. Originally, the clause was interpreted to cover only interstate commerce (trade and commerce between two or more states). Over the years, however, federal courts have viewed it as also pertaining to intrastate commerce (trade and commerce within a single state).

The Taxing and Spending Clause

Another clause that proves to be controversial and open to widely differing interpretations is the Taxing and Spending Clause. It states that "Congress shall have power to lay and collect taxes, duties, imposts [a tax or duty], and excises, to pay the debts and provide for the common Defence and general welfare of the United States; but all Duties, Imposts, and Excises shall be uniform throughout the United States." This clause has been used by the federal government, with the support of the courts, to justify federal taxes, including income taxes, payroll taxes, and tariffs (taxes on imported goods). But the clause's vague wording about "general welfare" has inspired much political debate. Even the Federalists and Anti-Federalists argued over it. Madison insisted that the clause be interpreted narrowly, while Hamilton argued for a broad understanding of it. Madison felt taxes should only be raised for specific purposes of national importance, like providing for the military or funding the regulation of interstate commerce. Hamilton felt taxes could and should be raised for more general spending purposes as long as it would benefit the entire country, rather than one state or region only.

The Necessary and Proper Clause

The third clause that has raised constitutional questions concerning the division of power between federal and state governments is the Necessary and Proper Clause. It states, "Congress shall have power to make all laws which shall be necessary and proper for carrying into Execution the foregoing powers, and all other powers vested by this Constitution in the Government of the United States, or in any Department or Office thereof." What exactly does "necessary and proper" mean? These terms are so vague that they can be interpreted to mean many different things. In fact, they are so generic that this clause is nicknamed the Elastic Clause because it can cover anything and everything. The Necessary and Proper Clause has enabled Congress to claim virtually any power for itself that its members deem appropriate. Over the years, Congress has indeed used the clause to expand its power. How far the Elastic Clause can stretch before snapping is a question that is still unknown.

CHAPTER FOUR

The ROLES of FEDERAL and STATE GOVERNMENTS TODAY

America has changed dramatically since the Revolutionary War, and ideas about what a good government is and what different parts of the Constitution mean have changed as well. The delegates at the Constitutional Convention could never have imagined how the United States and its people would change over the centuries. Neither could they have anticipated how historical developments would alter the effect of older laws and make necessary new ones to account for changing times and conditions. Perhaps if they could, they would have been more clear about what exactly they meant. But then again, perhaps not, one of the amazing things about our Constitution is its ability to express the goals and limits of the government even after so much has changed.

Due to its ambiguous wording, the Tenth Amendment continues to be one of the parts of the Constitution that inspires the most controversy and debate. There is a reason one of the biggest divisions between today's two major political parties is the role and size of the federal government. Contemporary issues like gun ownership, health care, environmental standards, the death penalty, medical marijuana, same-sex marriage, and assisted suicide all hinge upon the Constitution's division between federal powers and states' rights.

Some of these issues, like same-sex marriage, have become less and less contentious as time goes on. Others, like the legalization of marijuana, remain legally disputed but practically tend in one direction. Still others, like gun control, seem as though they will be controversial, hotly contested issues forever. The tense push-pull between the federal government and the states continues as each side tries to establish, defend, and expand its authority.

THE FAILURE OF NO CHILD LEFT BEHIND

In 2002, the No Child Left Behind Act (NCLB) was passed by President George W. Bush. The act promised education funding to states, but the money came with strings attached. NCLB mandated that federal funding for education would be given only to those states that developed and administered a basic skills test for students in specific grades. States whose students did not score high enough would lose funding. Those whose students excelled would receive more money. This policy was designed to ensure that educators were teaching

STATES' RIGHTS AND CIVIL RIGHTS

Though states of course have many rights, guaranteed by the Tenth Amendment, the phrase "states' rights" has some not-so-nice connotations. Since the 1940's, the term "states' rights" has become a kind of code word for anti-civil rights beliefs, because in the past, arguments for states' rights have been wielded to cut down federal laws about civil rights issues like racial desegregation and same-sex marriage. In fact, the short-lived National States' Rights Party was founded in 1958 as a white supremacist party. Segregation was a major issue in the struggle between civil rights and states' rights, as many states wanted to continue to segregate public places even as the federal government ruled that it was wrong. Likewise, states argued that they should not be required to recognize same-sex marriages performed in other states because it is a "state's right" to define marriage how it wants. Yet as we have seen, the states' rights argument can also benefit advocates for things like same-sex marriage, as it was part of the national conversation about DOMA that was discussed in the introduction.

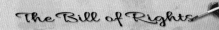

The Bill of Rights

the necessary skills and subjects in their classrooms and their students were learning them adequately.

While some state departments of education objected to NCLB on the basis of its unconstitutionality, still others

Though now widely considered a failure, No Child Left Behind initially seemed like a good way to make sure American students were learning all they were meant to each year of school. Unfortunately, it put a lot of focus on standardized tests, which inconvenienced already-overworked teachers and forced them to "teach to the test" rather than ensuring their students actually learned worthwhile material.

complained about the high cost of developing and administering the tests. Although federal funding was provided to help pay for these costs, it did not begin to cover the total bill. Bruce Hunter, spokesperson for the American Federation of

Teachers, applauds the intentions of the bill, yet still believes it to be unconstitutional. "Education is a state and local matter," he explains in an interview with Education World. "This enlarged the federal government's role to one that is unneeded and unnecessary . . . At some point, you give up something precious if you let the federal government tell the states and local government how to assess schools."

In 2009, NCLB was augmented by President Barack Obama's Race to the Top (RTTT) program, in which the former president promised $4.35 billion in grant money to schools that meet certain educational standards. While the money would be appreciated by all school systems, in order to get it, they would have to teach only what the US Department of Education deemed fit. Many people, from principals and city council members to parents and students, felt this was an example of the federal government intruding in areas better left to state and local policy makers. RTTT did encourage a number of states to adapt common national standards, but it could not really solve any of the issues of NCLB.

By 2015, the act had been so heavily criticized from all sides that Congress removed all national aspects of the act and replaced it with the Every Student Succeeds Act, which turned power over to the states. The Every Student Succeeds Act did keep many of the ideas of NCLB regarding standardized tests, and in that way reaffirms the federal government's role in funding public education, as outlined in the 1965 Elementary and Secondary Education act. Decisions regarding the specifics of educational reform, however, now belong to the states.

GUN CONTROL, STATE BY STATE

The right to bear arms is protected by the Second Amendment to the US Constitution. However, who can and can't own a gun, what kind of gun they can own, and how and when they can buy a gun are complicated and unresolved questions. The Brady Bill and other gun control legislation has put limits on gun ownership as well as on interstate weapons commerce.

In late 2009, the state of Montana signed a new law that stated in part that "a personal firearm, a firearm accessory, or ammunition that is manufactured commercially or privately in Montana and that remains within the borders of Montana is not subject to federal law or federal regulation, including registration, under the authority of Congress to regulate interstate commerce." In other words, any gun made entirely within the state and kept within the state would not be required to be registered by a gun buyer. Nor would gun sellers be required to run background checks on buyers of Montana-manufactured guns or keep records of the sales of these guns. The federal Bureau of Alcohol, Tobacco, Firearms, and Explosives (ATF) told

This is the seal of the federal Bureau of Alcohol, Tobacco, Firearms, and Explosives, which regulates the sales and sometimes the use of such substances and materials.

Montana that all federal gun regulations continue to apply, despite the passage of this state law.

Gary Marbut, who is president of the Montana Shooting Sports Association, said in response, "We feel very strongly that the federal government has gone way too far in attempting to regulate a lot of activity that occurs only in-state. It's time for Montana and her sister states to take a stand against the bullying federal government, which the legislature and governor have done and we are doing with this lawsuit." Other states followed Montana's example, including Texas, Arkansas, South Carolina, and Florida.

THE ISSUE OF LEGALIZING MARIJUANA

The legalization of marijuana is an issue that gets at the heart of the Tenth Amendment. It is illegal under federal law to use, own, sell, or grow marijuana, yet the drug is legal in certain capacities in many states, and the federal government has ruled that a state may decriminalize the drug with certain restrictions. One of the reasons that marijuana remains illegal on the federal level is that it is incorrectly listed as a Schedule I substance under the Controlled Substances Act of 1970, meaning that it supposedly has a high potential of being abused and that it cannot be used for medical purposes. However, marijuana is used for medical purposes across the country and therefore by definition should not be a Schedule I substance.

In 1996, California became the first state in the United States to legalize medical marijuana. Today, a majority of the states have legalized marijuana for medical purposes, like

like managing chronic pain and dealing with side effects of treatments like chemotherapy. Many states have begun to legalize it for recreational use. Even though it remains illegal on a federal level, it looks like someday very soon, marijuana will be very like alcohol: a legal drug used by adults for relaxation and, in the case of marijuana, for medical purposes as well.

THE TENTH AMENDMENT MOVING FORWARD

Other cases about the question of federal versus states' rights pop up across the country regularly, and most likely will keep doing so. Some of the issues being reviewed by federal courts today include environmental standards and requirements, the death penalty, and assisted suicide. Passionate debate on these issues ranges from what should and should not be legal to who gets to decide the answer in the first place—the federal government or the individual states.

When the framers of the Constitution drafted this history-changing document more than two hundred years ago, they had no way of foreseeing how society and its most pressing issues would evolve. They did, however, know how important independence, autonomy (self-government), and individual rights were to all human beings. When considering these questions we need to think long and hard about what kind of government we believe is best for America today, just like the Founding Fathers. As American citizens, it is our duty to be active in our government and our communities. We can be the Founding Parents of a new American government for the twenty-first century.

THE BILL OF RIGHTS

First Amendment (proposed 1789; ratified 1791): Freedom of religion, speech, press, assembly, and petition

Second Amendment (proposed 1789; ratified 1791): Right to bear arms

Third Amendment (proposed 1789; ratified 1791): No quartering of soldiers in private houses in times of peace

Fourth Amendment (proposed 1789; ratified 1791): Interdiction of unreasonable search and seizure; requirement of search warrants

Fifth Amendment (proposed 1789; ratified 1791): Indictments; due process; self-incrimination; double jeopardy; eminent domain

Sixth Amendment (proposed 1789; ratified 1791): Right to a fair and speedy public trial; notice of accusations; confronting one's accuser; subpoenas; right to counsel

Seventh Amendment (proposed 1789; ratified 1791): Right to a trial by jury in civil cases

Eighth Amendment (proposed 1789; ratified 1791): No excessive bail and fines; no cruel or unusual punishment

Ninth Amendment (proposed 1789; ratified 1791): Protection of unenumerated rights (rights inferred from other legal rights but that are not themselves coded or enumerated in written constitution and laws)

Tenth Amendment (proposed 1789; ratified 1791): Limits the power of the federal government

Bibliography

Delisio, Ellen. "No Child Left Behind: What It Means to You." *Education World*, June 24, 2002. http://www.educationworld. com/a_issues/issues273.shtml.

Denniston, Lyle. "Constitution Check: Did the Supreme Court take away states' power over marriage?" *Constitution Daily*, September 8, 2015. http://blog.constitutioncenter. org/2015/09/constitution-check-did-the-supreme-court-take-away-states-power-over-marriage.

Epps, Garrett. "U.S. v. Bond: Reexamining the Mysterious 10th Amendment." *The Atlantic*, February 28, 2011. http://www. theatlantic.com/national/archive/2011/02/us-v-bond-reexamining-the-mysterious-10th-amendment/71436.

Lively, Donald. *Landmark Supreme Court Cases*. Santa Barbara, CA: Greenwood Press, 1999.

Romero, Anthony. "Opposing View: Repeal Real ID." *USA Today*, March 6, 2007. http://www.usatoday.com/news/ opinion/2007-03-05-opposing-view_N.htm.

"10th Amendment: Rights Reserved to States or People." *Constitution Daily*, February 10, 2014. http://blog. constitutioncenter.org/2014/02/10th-amendment-rights-reserved-to-states-or-people-2.

"Understanding the 10th Amendment." *Laws.com*, 2017. Retrieved November 18, 2016. http://constitution.laws. com/american-history/constitution/constitutional-amendments/10th-amendment.

Utah State Legislature. "Resolution Opposing Real ID Act." Retrieved November 18, 2016. http://le.utah.gov/~2007/bills/hbillenr/hr0002.htm.

Woods, Thomas, and Kevin Gutzman. *Who Killed the Constitution? The Federal Government vs. American Liberty from World War I to Barack Obama.* New York, NY: Three Rivers Press, 2009.

Glossary

amendment A change or addition made to a legal document.

Anti-Federalists Opponents of federalism, or a strong central government.

biometric Describing technology that allows for the recognition and identification of individuals based on physical or behavioral traits, such as fingerprints; DNA; face, retina, and iris recognition; gait; and voice.

contentious Likely to cause a disagreement.

delegate A person authorized or sent to speak and act for others; a representative at a convention.

dictatorship A country, government, or form of government in which absolute power is held by a dictator, or supreme leader.

due process Fair treatment under the law.

interpret To explain the meaning of; to make understandable; to bring out the meaning of; to give one's own conception of something.

interstate business Commerce between states within a country.

preamble An introductory statement, preface, or introduction.

ratify To confirm by expressing consent, approval, or formal sanction.

republic A state in which the head of government is not a monarch or other hereditary head of state. Instead the people of the nation choose their leaders and have some role or representation or say in their government.

secede To withdraw formally from an alliance, federation, or association.

Further Reading

BOOKS

Baskin, Nora Raleigh. *Nine, Ten: A September 11 Story.* New York, NY: Atheneum Books for Young Readers, 2016.

Frith, Margaret. *Who Was Franklin Roosevelt?* New York, NY: Grosset & Dunlap, 2010.

Krull, Kathleen, and Anna DiVito. *A Kids' Guide to America's Bill of Rights.* Revised edition. New York, NY: HarperCollins, 2015.

Quirk, Anne, and Elizabeth Baddeley. *The Good Fight: The Feuds of the Founding Fathers (and How They Shaped the Nation).* New York, NY: Knopf Books for Young Readers, 2017.

WEBSITES

American Law Institute
http://www.ali.org

The American Law Institute is one of the leading independent legal organizations in the United States. The institute is made up of four thousand lawyers, judges, and law professors and drafts, discusses, revises, and publishes work that exerts a strong influence on courts and legislatures, legal scholarship, and legal education.

National Archives and Records Administration
http://www.archives.gov

The National Archives and Records Administration houses the Declaration of Independence, the Articles of Confederation, the Constitution, the Bill of Rights, the Emancipation Proclamation, and the Louisiana Purchase agreement along with other documents of national importance.

Tenth Amendment Center
http://www.tenthamendmentcenter.com

The Tenth Amendment Center is a national think tank that works to preserve and protect the principles of strictly limited government through information, education, and activism. The center serves as a forum for the study and exploration of state and individual sovereignty issues, focusing primarily on the decentralization of federal government power.

Index